Love Took the Words

Love Took the Words

Poems

CHRISTOPHER JANE CORKERY

SLANT

LOVE TOOK THE WORDS
Poems

Slant
An Imprint of Wipf and Stock Publishers
199 W. 8th Ave., Suite 3
Eugene, OR 97401

www.wipfandstock.com

HARDCOVER ISBN: 978-1-7252-6422-9
PAPERBACK ISBN: 978-1-7252-6421-2
EBOOK ISBN: 978-1-7252-6423-6

Cataloguing-in-Publication data:

Names: Corkery, Christopher Jane.

Title: Love took the words: poems / Christopher Jane Corkery.

Description: Eugene, OR: Slant, 2020.

Identifiers: ISBN 978-1-7252-6421-2 (paperback) | ISBN 978-1-7252-6422-9 (hardcover) | ISBN 978-1-7252-6423-6 (ebook)

Subjects: LCSH: Poetry. | American poetry. | American poetry — 21st century. | Elegiac poetry, American. | Grief — Poetry.

Classification: LCC PS3553.O6477 C6 2020 (print) | LCC PS3553.O6477 (ebook)

Manufactured in the U.S.A.   OCTOBER 1, 2020

For Eamonn, and in memory of his father

Contents

3

4

I

AS IN THE DAYS OF THE PROPHETS

Love took the words right out of my mouth.
Not the making of love, the clinging and plunge,
the tongue's deep spiral, but the acts of days,
the sun up and down, the dish and the pot,
the light on the head of first one, then another,
the stairs unswept, the bed made, the light out,
the papers brought in, the bed cold, the money
paid out, the bulbs dug, the children reverent
at what came next, the rise and the fall
of coral and ocher, the folding and sorting,
the endless numbering of things, the walking
with babies in slings, in backpacks, in strollers,
then hand in hand, then the hand dropped,
and one of them next to my shoulder, eyeing
before I do, the hawk or the waxwing,
the junco, the hermit thrush in the depths
of our gun-shot city, and just to the south
the great hill we climb, by season, together,
alone, in pairs, in trios, the slapping
of mud from our shoes on the back steps again,
the chastening memory of the otter plunging
in the icy water of his adequate tank
at the base of that hill. And love made the otter,
love made the mud, the ice-slicked bark,
the meals, the shining heads, and the sleep,
the risings, the children, the hawk's spiral.
Love took the words right out of my mouth.

HAPPINESS

The two-year old holds a broom, as if a guitar.
He is not far from a place in the stars
Where music is air, food, and water.
The two-year old plays his guitar

And feels the broomstraws brush his fingers.
One day he'll feel the curl and bristle
Of his girlfriend's hair. They'll sit, entwined,
By a river and watch, there, on the water

Swans twirl. It's only May
And the dark asters that will command
His grief in later years are only
Buds. He'll think he is a swan

Upon the water (for they are young).
And she, too, a swan, but something
More. Then that thing's gone, an air
Played, somewhere, under stars.

Yet where? For stars are everywhere.
And to some they always speak, and the man
Always will think, whenever he holds
His guitar, thus, between chest and arm,

Of his first happiness, of the girl, of his sure
Baby grip, and the flick of his fingers.
It was happiness, next to a window he could not
Yet see out of, but which his mother

Had polished, and left, full of stars.

THE STRAPS OF THEIR SANDALS

Who is my mistress?
Who leads me when only
Rubble is left, fragments,
We say, three words or four?
Klio your sandal
But what if
Klio your sandal
Is as beautiful as
The small white statue
Of Zeus that the other
Poets have honored
Klio my verse
Will save you forever
Your thick hair the color
Of Patmos's olives
Your skin as pale
As the sands of Delos

I lay there, a woman
Of the twentieth century.
I was white as a bone,
My life seemed as small
As a grain of sand,
And it was, and it is.
I have borne children, two sons,
Loved a daughter.
Will they be fodder?
Be found, millennia hence,

Bronzed, as corpses
A poet could sing,
Trapped in miasms of lava,
And no one to know
The sturdy beauty
Of their hands and their feet,
The straps of their sandals,
Their bodies lithe
And trusting, their eyes
As brown as the olives of Patmos,
Their ready laughter astounded
When sorrow came in and nailed to a tree
The wordless articles of evil?

CENTRAL AND MAIN

The little old woman
(She is just that)
Whose skin is pale,
Yellow from lack
Of love, of sun
(From age, in short)
Who's wrapped in plaid
Her mother wore,
Has crossed the street
To the library's door.

She brings back *The Pearl*
(Pleasure for princes!)
Which her sister translated
Decades ago,
But also has under
Her elbow the News-
Letter of the Ladies
Of the Holy Trinity.
She knows how death
Has brought two
To their knees today
And knows, without
An allegory,
What comfort (little),
Can be given.

The other woman
Who has crossed at the same
Time is alert
To other signals.
Her lips are the color
Of red plums,
Her skirt the gauze
Of moth wings,
Her blouse shines
And through it the supple
Swing of her breasts
Makes red rise up
The throat of Mr.
Wilson, at the corner,
Who also crosses,
Who also dreams,
Who loses his purpose
Near the Bon Marché.

Now bright cars mosey
Through the intersection
Of Central and Main
Having stopped for him,
For her, and even
For the old woman.
The fall air
Is bracing, the sun
Is full gold,
Yet each one knows,
Somehow, what's blowing,
Brewing, coming.
Oh life, says each—
Three spirits receptive
As Marconi's first

Continent-kissing waves—
Oh life,
Let it be me
Who's here forever!

THE WOMAN AT THE TIJUANA DUMP

With thanks to Luis Alberto Urrea

The Madams of the Sacred Heart
taught me cartography,
the basic laws of limit, border,
(the first, as far as you could go,
the second, as far as they let you)
and tricks of colored water to give them body—
but never how to understand disaster
except as suffering, inevitable,
like drops of blood that Jesus shed for us.
Perhaps he did, and only in brutal slaughter
is evil understood—not understood,
but suffered once by God so all who suffer
can see he did it too, took on the blasted
face and scabrous body of the poor,
the leaping, skinny steps of the man who runs
along, and then across the wire if he's lucky.

"If you are king, come down from there!"—
a reasonable request, I think,
but he would not, the unreason of his life
making him a creature of the border,
being that stands as mystery and monument,
as does the woman in the Tijuana dump
who spoke as a god when the visitor asked her if
he might take home a shiny thing as artifact.

She was sturdy, this woman in acid-frayed boots
blue sweatpants, a stained purple shirt.
She wore rubber gloves and she opened her arms
wide, as she turned around and said
Of course, this is the dump, there is enough
for all.

JIGSAW PUZZLE IN PREGNANCY

Here is a beginning to harmony and peace.
All tidy on the little farm?
Are all the farmers sleeping?

See how the miles of rock-piled fence
Divide the too-green hillside.
Where are the pigs? Where are the cows?
Why is the sky so wide?

The pink fits in but the grey confounds.
The water stands still. From heat? From grief?
How many haycocks make a farm?
Whose is the shadowy face at the door?

The little inlet of salty water
Lies like an island behind the house.
Yellow flowers stud the hedges.
Was famine ever a problem at all?

Thatched roof, white wash, veneer of order,
Veneer of calmness, but inside
The kettle's not on the boil. Why should I
Learn what it means to stand at the door?

The mountains have sat like that for years,
Tilting their way to the waterside.
The splotch on the hill? The rich man's house.
He has taken a young girl for his bride.

Shall I ride out and tell her to come
To the cottage below, with its meager store?
Could they sit? Would bread cool on the table?
Of what would they talk? The most recent war?

I fit in more pink (there's been a storm),
But the lake's still flat and the grey confounds.
O women in mourning on hillside, in valley,
Whose is the shadowy face at the door?

THE CHOSEN

Child, whose mother gives you up
Now into another's arms,
You will find your second home
Stunning in its swathe of love.

But *Who was it?* you'll come to ask,
Who carried me on shining water?
What taut muscle was the wall
Between my self and earth's pain?

Mother, Father, love me dearly.
On this dark path they are my guides.
But who was that who first was world?
Who fed me yellow drops of light?

Life's wild country is more seen
Each day by me, omnivore.
Barranca, prairie, bricked-up alley—
Which was the landscape that she wore?

Memory, they say, cannot
Reach where mine has always gone.
Fingers stroke my brow and lips,
First light is equal to the song

Sung to me when I emerged,
First a shudder, then that breath.
I walk in company all life long
With her whose loss was my first death.

PATIO

I count the bricks
(Each pairing clicks),
Count the space
I need to make
To hold four chairs,
A plate of pears,
And a table of wood
On which the plate
Can sit.

To this green shade
I won't admit
Defeat, or heat,
Or an angry clock
Outraged at having
No time to tell,
Or love embarrassed
Because unanswered,
Or men political
And thick.

Bricks and dirt,
Sand and shade,
The thirsty maples
Still in our service—
Is this how the word
Turns into flesh,
No paten raised

But a summer yard,
One child hiding
Deep in forsythia,
The other boldly
Waiting to be born.

UPHOLSTERY

I love to say *upholstery*—what a ridiculous word!—
conjuring *uphold* and *holsters*, Poles
who've held me, bras and jock-straps holding up,
leather straps from subway crossbars
the summer of sixty-six, the sweat at eighty-ninth,
then all gets smeared to *hostelry*
and that brings always Bess, the landlord's daughter,
the musket at her breast, *tlot-tlot, tlot-tlot,*
the first spilt sound of vowels for me,
and blood I did not know was literary.
But then I turn away for there are real
murders, daily, near the street where I live, and love,
the comical *pop pop pop* of real guns.

These are the streets where the upholsterer lives
a plain and simple life, as in Barbados,
he says, except he has two guns and says
that if they come, he will be ready.
The last remnant he unearthed was unicorns
on a red field, the huntress crowned, rampant.
These are the streets where the Reverend Johnson lives
who holds the chalice up (a thing I never
did, but longed to do, the surplice sibilant
on my shoulders). The first child I beheld
I lay down to bring into this world,
the second I stood up for, upheld
by my husband. Now I hold these pages up
but only for a moment. Though light might show

a water-mark, I'd rather hand them to you thus.
I am Daedalus's daughter, rescued by my trade,
Come. Rest on the couch I've made.
It holds up well.

ALMOST STILL LIFE

Under the wings of the angel begonia
Nothing is silvered. The leaf is dark red.

Thistle stands in an ivory pitcher,
the curve of its handle blue in the shadow.

Above us, on the wall, a woman holds a cherry.
She is framed in gray, the cherry is dark red.

A minuscule balloon, tied to her thumb,
is smaller than the cherry. Pale. Almost white.

My skin is white, like the meat of an apple.
Your skin is brown, like the river's throat.

In the dark, the cherry slips from her fingers.
We split it between us. The skin is dark red.

A cry, then a silence. The angel begonia's
Leaves are all shadow. Love lights our bed.

DREAM AND PRÉCIS

Rosie put the saucer down
Thinking to put milk in it.
Lester tipped the saucer then,
To see the rivers on the floor.
Fred swept the whole thing up,
Into the dented metal pan,
Hearing Mother's different voice,
The thing behind it blue, like rain.

Rosie died before she was born.
Fred is grown, and Lester's gone.
Their mother is older, every day,
Less of a child, some songs begun.

2

MARCH

After Chaucer's *Mercilesse Beautie*

I

It was March, not a time of heat
In these parts, yet. No steam to undo
The straitened heart. No swallows blue

Lifting the meadows. "If we happen to meet,"
I thought on my walk, "I'll ask if his love grew."
    But it was only March, not a time of heat
    In these parts yet, no steam to undo.

And it wasn't in the meadows, nor on a street
I'd see him again. Everything is new,
Now, for me; it must be. No more blue.
    And it's only March, not a time of heat
    In these parts yet, no steam to undo
    The straitened heart, no swallows blue.

2

I've faced it: it was simply beauty took me.
Eyes, the smooth skin, the deft hands:
These are what the heart understands.

When you're young, it's clear: truth *is* beauty.
None of us, young, wants to avoid its brand.

I've faced it: it was beauty, simply, took me.
Eyes, smooth skin, the deft hands.

No matter where we walked, how faithfully
He took my part, listened to what I'd planned—
I should have known truth cannot expand.
    I've faced it now: it was simply beauty took me,
    Eyes, the smooth skin, deft hands.
    These tangibles the heart understands.

3

Finally, finally, I let go
That ghostly prey. I let it run for cover.
Not one more shade would I take for lover.

I crossed out the name of love's alter ego,
I threw out all the pages once pored over.
    Finally, finally, I let go
    That ghostly prey. I let it run for cover.

As for real love, I now, certain, know
Its name, dimensions; there's nothing to discover
Beyond your continent. The quest is over.
    Finally I did it. Finally I let go
    All ghostly prey. I let it run for cover
    Not one more shade would I take for lover.

A SCRAP OF FABRIC AT CHATHAM

The waves' surrender on the south shore
and an uninhabited old house
made you put on a palely striped tie
sent from Rangpur, a clean white shirt,
a navy blue suit—wasn't it that?—
and we began to dance in a cold interior
like that of dreams, until a thousand pink
butterflies launched themselves, wings sticky,
and the dialogue I have only imagined began,
that clear conversation spoken by souls
meant, longing to bear each other's presence.

THINGS

Hello, says the paper.
Hello, the hat.
Pick me up, read me,
Put me on.

We wait with the clock,
And the kettle, and the long
Breadknife whose handle
Is silky with age.

Use us, walk on
To the world's stage.
Learn that you
Are an actor as well.

Of kindness? Revenge?
Who can tell?
Of a subtler love?
Choose. Choose.

The breadboard is round,
The color of cloves.
A lovely bevel
Travels its edge

And the word Bread—
Who incised it?—
Turns and returns,
As if things were simple.

IT WAS YEATS WHO TOOK ME

It was Yeats who took me. I was seventeen,
In love with watery consonants, with boys.
But Yeats would show me what my life could mean.

Afraid of men, yet drawn, a sucker for looks,
I studied his dark forelock, his sweet mouth.
It was Yeats who took me, I was seventeen.

My best friend's boy, another bow-lipped wonder,
Took me for screaming rides on a Norton 850.
But Yeats would show me what my life would mean.

I talked the boyfriend silly, held off advances
Until the time I couldn't. And yet, and yet. . . .
It was Yeats who took me! I was seventeen

And ready to believe words spoken to shells,
Because he was so lonely, like me, so weird.
Yeats would show me what my life could mean.

I clung to that great body. His delight
In love, and loss, and water, and swans was mine!
It was Yeats who took me, (I was seventeen),
And showed me, word by word, what life could mean.

GALAXIES

I

Off to Ireland at twenty-four
I sought an entry, a kind of door
Into the past I'd heard bits of
For all those years. My mother's love
Had circled stories of hedge schools,
The penal laws, the pack of fools
Who gave away the six counties.
And Daniel Corkery's hidden bounties.

So, I began to study Yeats.
Words alone are certain good, he said,
And though he spoke it to a shell,
I understood. He knew me well,
That aristo so different from my own,
Knew, as I did, a huckster when he saw one.
I'd come from this, love and a kind of frenzy
To blue the edge of loss, the knife of envy.
Words alone were certain good. A poem, a story
Could see a child through a month of worry.
Repeat, repeat, the flowing verbs, the nouns.
Those people at it in the other room, I'd say,
Are not my own.

2

Now, when I see their faces in my mirror
Or hear their favorite lines of flight and rapture—
"I fled him down the nights and down the days,"
"Build thee more stately mansions, O my soul,"
I know just how early I was meant for
Longing that was hinged on more than nation,
Hound and nautilus images of belonging
To a home I'd either run from, or was building.

3

And would my mother have had me read
The man I later read, William Carleton?
An aging, crazed academic said
I had to read these books whose pages no one
Had even cut, much less taken to bed.
With student somnolence at first, but then
With open eyes, I read what he was forced
To write, having seen. Ferocious, double-sided,
small-minded, then large- and absolutely
Clear as to particulars of greed,
Venality, cruelty, as over and over again
He verified his details of disgust—
Bodies rotting on the road, and bodies
Swinging from British gibbets, bagged in sacks
That dripped with tar and hate. It was 1845,
After all. I read and read.

4

And when I saw the invasion of the Bogside
On television, in 1969,
Not sixty miles from where each shot was fired,

I was in Sligo with a bunch of would-be poets.
A few were real. The air stank of stout,
And smoke, and sweat, and we were futile members
Of the human body, all our waste exposed.

Beside inert men, I too was inert,
A member of the mystical body of Yeats,
Condemned, it seemed, to know his lines by heart.
We might as well have been in the far Bermudas,
For all the heat in the pub, and for the little
We let his weird prowess power us.
What planet were we citizens of that night
Who sat, all still, and watched as children fell?

5

To enter Trinity College Dublin
One passed the Bank of Ireland
Which had been the Irish Parliament,
Cesspool and seat of fashion.
Inside College Gate
(these were the seventies)
Worker-students foamed at the mouth,
And calling Yeats a fascist,
They bade me read no more.

6

A year later in a laundromat off Baggott Street
I watched the summer roads the rain had drenched
While my lover was leaving me, literally,
High-stepping out of the laundromat and saying,
That was that. His reproach: that I was not his wife.
I couldn't fault him there.

7

O take me back to that wide road,
To the Clyde Road in late spring,
With fuschia budlets waving
And cherry blossoms blowing
On the little Chinese maiden
In the charming architect's garden!

In the North a girl's knees were being shattered
For her talking to a Brit. I thought of a girl
Like me, as I had been at twelve or fourteen,
Fear my ruler. I wouldn't kiss a cat.
I thought of her boldness, heat, and need.

At twice her age I was holding wet laundry
And thinking what mattered was a man from Perth
Who played at being revolutionary.
Socks and wet towels hung from my arms,
And the Bogside was nothing, as Tet had been nothing,
While I hurtled, unknowing, through the galaxies of self.

TO FIND A WAY TO THE WORLD'S HEART

A simple way, as simple as the table
at which George Herbert sat (his view of the river
unobscured, new catkins rising,
his view of his own sins hugely blinkered),
or that at which Teresa ate
her bread and meat and wine (two plates,
one goblet, all of tin) after a day
of meeting with the bishop, then selling thirty hectares
she would much rather have kept, for they were orchard,
then instructing novices in submission,
which is an art that one must pray for
and must practice well before the prayer is answered;

the candlesticks before her are intricately chased
with wreaths and crosses, and polished to a glare.
She has no pity for herself, but for a world
as beautiful as the one beyond her shutters,
even now, with the fields stripped of grain,
that gold turned to gray, and the winds rough from Toledo,
a world stunning but for its poor guardians,
whose hearts are lashed by doubt,
who have married complication.

THE FIRST TO MAKE MUSIC

Can this be my poem to nature?
How I'd think it a death if I could not, again,
watch a chickadee feed its young by diving,
first, down the hollow trunk of an old lilac,
how I need the buzz of the racket of the nuthatch,
and the yellow-striped salute of the Carolina Wren
outside our bedroom? There's nothing sweet about it,
just *Here! Here! Here!* And if you believe
In the body's resurrection, then you believe
in music's eternal life. And the first to make music—
aside from the lovers whose cries, shock-bright,
were dulled as their makers became aware of
loneliness—that music could be lonely—
the first were the birds, like the Red Phalarope
deemed "out of place" in a dry New England marsh,
immature, and busy, and robust, pinkish,
noticed as he would not be in a flock
paprika-ing a whole, vast, Alaskan bay,
although there it's the totality that stuns,
generation's mammoth blush.
And if the resurrection eludes you or defeats you,
you'd best get up and look, look up, and see
if, through the veil of rain, high up
in that white pine's cover you can still detect the shape
of a napping owl. If not, there is no music
but the breath of the beast of greed we all contain.

TEACHING *TO THE LIGHTHOUSE*

How hard they work at finding out
what was meant when X was said.

The young women are in love
with Mrs. Ramsay, are in love

with some slight ghost of what might happen.
But only some of the young men

are thus seduced, as was young Tansley
whose neck was red where he had scrubbed

too hard, whose collar's dirty,
Rose observed, shrinking.

O Rose, you silent fruit arranger,
you shadow girl, of Mother's jewels

the chooser and the changer!
How girls love the dear setting out,

inventing style, coaxing color, fanning
into parabola the curls on Mother's neck,

a shape both ancient and suggestive
and one that Mrs. Ramsay would not admit

to having seen in a common magazine.
It's rather like arranging here

what's dear, and lost, or there
in a pale classroom, making clear

the presence of a past not analogue,
of the ghosts of men cut down along the Somme

who chant in every reader's dream, and Rose's,
the sustenance of truly chosen things.

BY OURSELVES

Write a poem about a playground, my mother said.
An empty playground where the swings are swinging
By themselves. That's one I've never read.

My own son flew by himself, heels over head.
He sang a song called "How Can I Keep From Singing?"
Write a poem about a playground, my mother said.

Some stories are the ones by which we're led
As if by a shining moon, or orioles, singing,
To ourselves. But there's one I've never read.

It tells of a girl who's strong and feels no dread
Of her soul's high flight, or of death, stinging.
Write a poem about a playground, my mother said.

Look at a schoolyard one July, she said,
Where chipped green swings that live to fly are struggling
By themselves. That's one I've never read.

She missed her babies. She felt a quickened dread.
She called to them, but they were grown, not listening.
Write a poem about a playground, my mother said.
Call it "By Ourselves." That's one I've never read.

DECLARATIVE

So much time passed.
And any change?
Any true effort
such as forklifts, front-end loaders,
back-hoes accomplish?
Steered by us, true, made by us,
fashioned in our image of push, shove, dump.
But there's silence at the end of the day
when all the muscled boys go home
and they, too, face questions that
they can't escape. It's at the pub
or at their ma's or at the pounding
into someone. What? What?
What? And, Why? Or Keats's simpler,
towards the end: "I don't understand."

BEHIND THE HOUSE

At the turning where sumac will redden and fade
a solitary kinglet cocks her head,
her half-ringed eye half-question.
Though water flows nearby and a haze of maples
replicates the haze of love's compulsion,
the scene is mostly dense with leaves,
and high in the fretwork an oriole's nest,
which I desired once to be the builder of,
is swinging.

        Nothing is owned,
and the light that turns the Indigo Bunting blue
washes our entanglement as well.
O prophet of the morning walk,
of worlds demolished and peoples disappeared,
tell me it is not little courage we have displayed so far.

3

REPOSITORY

We never went to the pool in Florence,
but I thought in the hills, where a ghost of you
took in honeycomb, the net on your hat
so grey it could not be told from the leaves—

I thought how pleasant it would be to descend at will,
as gods can do, and swim our laps
next to the river, the children riding plastic ducks
where torrents had risen and carried holy books.

"Do you want *gelati?*" I would cry to the boys
but they would not answer until later,
when they'd shaken the gold drops from their backs
and stared at San Miniato's brilliants.

We were storing love in our cells for a reason.

DANTE CONFUSES US

Dante confuses us on purpose in the *Vita Nuova*.
He does not care. Because he is great he has confidence.
In his method, in his choice. He says, *this happened then,*
and, *Later, I wrote this down.*

It was always she, but also always he, noting and
recording, and, being a linguist in the deepest sense,
considering how to re-embody what his body knew.
In words. In shape. And explanation: that had

to be part of it. He did not care
if he were understood immediately. He knew
his process was correct. Full of himself he under-
stood the weight of love, and word. He waited
until she was years gone and then began
to piece it together, to feel God's love as motive.

WHEN YOUR DAUGHTER WAS TURNING
TWENTY-EIGHT

When your daughter was turning twenty-eight
I began a sestina,
that box-like wonder
of words, of let-in light.
It was an exercise only, but I thought—
Better the intended, than the forgotten

Gift. In the library, chores forgotten,
(it was in Milton, Rte. 28)
worry, disappointment too; I thought
the formed sugar of a sestina,
that transparent cage of light,
might inform my incorporeal wonder

As to where I found myself: no real wonder
was inside me then. Our younger ones away, I had forgotten
how I came to be where I was—had flight
or purpose brought me to Rte. 28?—
its tangible oak table, tangible sestina
demanding a more strict thought,

An honester reckoning. I thought
it was for her, but no. I wonder
how many lives a toiled-over sestina
can hold? Few, it seems: I had forgotten
the enormity of the ego. Even Rte. 28
a bland road, dully formed, forbade flight

From the self. The gold light
of the Languedoc would have been better, thought
anaesthetized by a Chenin haze, twenty-eight
years celebrated in Occitan wonder—
a curved street, a glass she might have drunk. I had forgotten
how much I loved that green sestina

of Dante's, the first time around, the sestina's
trobar clu—how green-gold light
could be pressed from suffering. Not forgotten,
really. But youth wants only to be touched, wants thought
to fade; that love wants only a body. Wonder
at that held me once. But now—she who once was twenty-eight

Has a daughter, twenty-three. Not thought, but wonder,
And grief are bound in the sestina. And of the light
At my first sight of you? Not one thing is forgotten.

REPLACEMENT

When I went to get a replacement for a large,
full journal, the Staples was not there.
Gone the S T A P L E S that had hung above the door;
left, the shadow of those letters, pale but present,
like the mustache of a thirteen year-old boy.

You are gone, really, with no trace, no letter
left for me to find, no last sonnet, no . . . .
Nothing but what you were, and I am; what we were.
But it fades, and I am horrified,
left standing in a shopping plaza, staring at the tracery of commerce,

thinking I will not escape this desert of the mind,
a mind that couples you, and S T A P L E S, then adds a third:
Proust falling—or was it simply tripping?—
and years later remembering the stumble
as a kind of healing. This does not happen to me.

NEAR HANSCOM AIR BASE

"Where is that *Paradise Lost?*" I awoke saying.
I meant of course your blue volume,
oddly sized, large and thin, perhaps 9" x 6"
and underlined in your last year of college
when you left the crowd, got your own room,
And read.

      The cover was a kind of blue
I love, but for which I cannot find a modifier.
Nor can I modify you, my life with you a sentence
whose diagram confounds—so many byways,
so many contingencies rising, falling, rising.

I knew nothing of love when we met.
What do I know now after your complex death?
It is quiet almost all the time in our house,
except for the drone of fighters, angling up from Hanscom.

BY THE OCEAN

My head is storms at morning
With all the things I've read.
And then at night my head is still.
And you are still dead.

My hipbone holds the weight
Of your forearm in sleep.
But waking I am alone, slight.
Jetsam from the deep.

Yours, a simple name. A lure
for me into the net
of safety, danger, sex, love—
And I do not know you yet!

Was I the pearl or you?
Were you, or I, the shell?
No answer no answer no answer
But the near buoy's bell.

PAINTER ON SCAFFOLDING IN SUMMER

Inside the house, all I can see
are the painter's legs from waist down.
And I am struck by his delicate ankles;
it is August, and hot, and he wears no socks.
On his feet old lace-up oxfords—
the elegance of it! Strong legs, and the barest
horizontal motions in the torso
as he edges clapboards. Back. Forth.

Why this seems hopeful I do not know.
Yet briefly, no one is sick, and fate
declines for this half-hour to announce a thing.
And I remember you standing at ease
after a race, the center of your chest moving,
not seeming to move.

THE SIREN

To a poet

The "thing-ness" of your poems impressed me.
By that I mean that many were the nouns
and that, among them, it seemed most were concrete
(unlike the previous line) and colorful, or colored—
The Lenten rose, the rotting meat, the lake,
Your lover's back, your father sleeping, old,
And, by inference, gray, in the adjacent room.

You, though, seemed to be on hold—
different from me, holding back, perhaps,
the thing that would crack you in two, the too-hard thing:
and here we move to me: my husband's right-hand fingers
scrabbling at his left, where his wedding ring
should be, and I, assuring him I had it.
That siren wailed for me.

TORN PAPER

1

Remember, remember, and not from the grave,
Our little flat in Paris, our bed's space
Like a ship's cubby, curtained, square, it barely
Fit us. But did. You in hard won recovery
From surgery: the one-lunged man!
You coughed, I coughed from cold, but we were one
In purpose: to survive, and watch, with care,
The raindrops slowly make their way
Down our glass door, the geraniums
Across the courtyard almost waving.
The gravel beds of the Jardin des Plantes
Contain, still, pebbles that we trod.
The mosque nearby watched us walk
With only a little stagger.

2

Street of the key, *Rue de la clef*, it was called.
I mispronounced that key for days, rhyming it
with deaf, that "ear" that I'd been praised for
disparu. So much had gone from us.
I stopped my walking every now and then
To wonder where we were, where I was
Who had assumed some things that were not:
How strong you were, how close we were,
How far away the Lady of the Unicorn.

Too far for you, I went alone
and laughed at the little dog but also thought—
This is no place for him, a dark room,
The woman sitting manless.

3

A tiny paper cup, one inch full
of espresso. That's what you brought me
from the tabac. I added sugar, an inch of milk,
Et in Arcadia . . . strange Arcady—
urban, the sky a torn bit of paper
in the door's high glass. My God,
the happiness love restarted brings!
Of course, it was always there, the way
a secret message is, deep in the page's calm,
until some hand rubs drops of acrid juice
across the sentence. Does the line use
the word, *love*, at all? Oh no, it says
"Forgive! Forgive! Forgive!"

4

THE OLD DAYS

Did we do the best we could? I asked you that, in absentia,
And you, occupied with finer things, could not answer.
I did not blame you then. I gave you flowers.

This barrier between the living and the not present—
As high as the blood-brain one baffling cancer?
I did not blame you then, I'd give you flowers

Now, the kind you most adored, tulips, and even phlox—
Though you did not lean at all to gardening. Denser
Than you, no blame, but still I'd give you flowers if I could,

By the truckload. And then a magic composting—
No guilt, but only regeneration and dancers
Circling, no blame but a fouetté of flowers

As in the old days of hallucinogens, a present
You had loved, in the old days. No answer
Was wrong. Each exhale made of flowers

One could not only smell, but eat. But that was you
Not me. Another type of human, I've been in a trance
For years. I'm stuck on keen, and what use flowers?

The bed is empty, the body that was ours
Half works. We did the best we could, of course,
But no one asks me questions now, nor answers.

THE FOLIAGE OF TULIPS

Brilliant sun this May first. In Cambridge
they were out by the river, those bearded Morris men, jingling,

and Morris ladies too. And in Mount Auburn now birders
are racing up and down the urn-ed slopes: they have to: it's freezing

and I, frozen in my heat-off house, have turned it on:
one whoosh of hot to take the edge off:

horror at being irresolute, still, as to where I am, and what:
in every thing I write disaster looming. Yet the dictionary

indicates no progression from "loom, a frame for weaving,"
to the hover-over-all immensity of Something Coming

which we cannot avoid. There must be a connection, though,
words' joints making sanity possible, society too, even the day.

Once you said I'd "salvaged the day." It had been by sex, this
salvage, nothing wrong with that, though it made me think of us

of us as wreck, sea-wrack attached. Let me note now the wrack
of the garden just eight weeks ago, and then the bulbs I planted

four weeks before you died—hyacinths and tulips—began to kick
themselves out of the ground. Hyacinths, dark purple, I

will always be true to, but: I hate the foliage of tulips.
Why this follows is the fact of nothing being pure but what we imagine:

the glow of a new, healthy tulip, fat, all color,
meeting its maker in the nano-second life of the mind's eye.

But look, the real one comes with the leathery decadent flop
of its real leaves, post-pop. I rip up every year that flesh,

rue not one bulb crushed by my demolishing,
so happy am I to make disappear, make not be,

assertions of inertia. But being alone now I
better understand what has to follow the astounding life,

the color. As with you: and subject to the infirmity of the tulip,
both of us. No firm may lead to no form but I no longer kid myself,

there was matter in your coming and going, matter
and spine and color beyond denial, and in the house, even now,

two children are playing Explore and one says he is Charles the Fifth,
and the other shouts "No! No! A pirate! A pirate!"

They could keep fighting over this, but do not, consumed as they are,
by the matter that they make.

IL CAVALLINO, LITTLE HORSE

How dangerous can it be to sit on a terrace
high on a hill near Doccia, which is silent as ever,
minding one's business, which is not much,
and thinking about the garden even higher
above the old, old house. . . .

how full it was
of rucola, how later the parmeggian'
thinly shaved over the top of the greens,
and redolent, would be finished by only drops
squeezed from a quarter lemon by your husband's hand.

That hand was brown, and long-fingered, graceful.
And the wrist as well—oh how these memories feed us
and starve us at the same time!

No danger though in remembering—surely no danger?
The now-dry spring that was called Il Cavallino,
at the bottom of a gully reached by our friends' dark path.

I got water from it, squatting by an old man
who said *"Prendi! Bevi!"* offering me one of his bottles.
He was old as any of the guardians of the sacred
yet, unlike many of those, he was kind.
Or perhaps he was like all of them in this:
face to face offering/demanding/saying:
"Drink! Take and drink. Do it now!"

KING PLEASURE, 1976

So much I wanted, then, to see my words.
To see my words. I wanted so much
In those days, that wanting was the essence

of being there. Wanting, you said. . .that's all man's life.
You said things like that. Why not? Yet,
with you, I was not wanting. Why were you?

To see my words again, to see my words—
why this fever, endless? I saw my words
on paper, dreamed them on papyri, dreamed

you, in a hazy palimpsest. But I was I,
not you. What was I looking for?
Enlightenment? A willful obfuscation?

I had no mad hopes, except
to see my words. No long accretion, but once
(and here you did not laugh) to see myself

beyond the want, beyond the desolation
of your going. Was it too much
or far, or little: my wish to see you whole

without your wants? To see my words without
desire? To go beyond geography—
where you grew up, where I—but never beyond

that place where we would meet:
two people on a corner, above their heads
and dangling by one metal bracket

(a sign too rusted to read)

and this is what I remember:
no lyre was involved at all.
But you were singing on that corner

a song about desire,
and you sang just like King Pleasure.
It was 1976.

WORLDS

Two just-fledged downy woodpeckers,
having found they can perch on the protruding ends
of the feeder's (dowel-less) dowel holder,

are, repeatedly, happy. They move from these
to my porch rail, and back. My naturalist friend
says I cannot say that—*happy*—but I do.

And the tiny bellies of these new-to-the-world
seem to want to be stroked by me. But no.
Worlds apart we remain: I, wishing I spoke

their speech, or could pass, as one just has,
a seed to the beak of another.

AT A CONVENT SCHOOL NORTH OF PARIS:

An orchard above which dormitory windows hung.
Eight of us leaned out those windows to suck in the air,
the richness of which, even to girls born there,
was *extraordinaire:* So that Caroline
(pronounce it Caro-*leen*) leaning further,
said I'm going, and managed to pull a tree top to her
And slip onto and down its feebler top branches
To the upholding V at its center.

High enough, she could not be brought down for a day,
not by shout nor imploring, nor the Reverend Mother's
hissed vow to expel. We, her friends, were jealous,
but also admiring. We watched her black hair be obscured
by blossoms. They were pear and white. So little to do
in tiny Gouvieux. So many myths to revise.

JOSEPHSVILLE

The sky seemed so gigantic in that hill country town
that I almost was seduced into buying a vast shell
of a dry goods store, "Estd. 1895,"
its old display shelves and cabinets shoved up
against walls, but visible the old way of work,
not free of larceny entirely, but permeable and
knowable to the merchant and the young man
who there bought his first tie, and what would
never seem to him an emblem of unrequited labor
was instead an outward sign of capital's inward
grace. My grandfather sold clothes in an elegant
department store much further west; each morning
a silk pocket handkerchief was the last thing he put on,
a quick look in the mirror confirming balance.

"HAWTHORN AND WAXWINGS"

In the hawthorn twelve cedar waxwings
Bounce and pluck berries that mimic
The scarlet of their wingtips. Is this art?
Whose were the palette and the brush
Is not the question, since Anon configured
Berries and birds, making us happy. "Ecstatic!"

Is the better word. (Nabokov loved the ecstatic
Dignity of the color, the busyness of the waxwing.
Why would he not, a master of configuring
Identities in mirrors, twin worlds mimicking
Perfectly love's plosive variations, his brush
Depicting much more than memory's art.)

Did the miniaturist call it Art?
Did it hide from her a long while, the way the ecstatic
Birds in winter do? Then, walking, did she come on brush
That turned, in a blink, to waxwings, a haze of waxwings
Working hard at those trembling berries, and, for her, mimicking
Ways we ward off death? Some do it by configuring,

On idle days, the gates of heaven, (where such figuring
Is past all use). Each is alone then. No art,
No priced estate will mean a thing there, nor mimicking
Saints' courage. (As for those ecstatic
Ways of going, that time has passed. Not even waxwings
Get in free.) The miniaturist lifted her brush

Even so, to make life, sometimes to brazenly brush
All she could into—*yes*—ornament! No configuring
Of forever moved her now. Making the waxwings
Was enough, almost, the blatant art
Of their bodies and flight, their blunt bills, their ecstatic
Sociability, their gauging eyes—not mimicking

An ideal. They *are* it—carmine, ocher, black, white—not mimicking
But being the palette she needs. The brush
Of the miniaturist, though, was never ecstatic
As it worked, but cool, and slow, configuring
How three, four, five, six colors could make art:
Living flames, called here "Hawthorn and Waxwings."

In it is no trace of the maker, her brush, or of mimicking.
Only this ecstatic configuring of waxwings,
And the breath of art that makes the hawthorn tremble.

BECAUSE THE NIGHT WAS BOISTEROUS, HAPPY, YOU

began to recite "Prufrock"   as we walked by the river
          not by any tour-boat dock   but further, upstream

where oranges,   the bitter Sevillanas,
          begged to be addressed   (the air wintry yet in Seville),

but we were busy   at the back and forth
          of recitation,   at our quick

excitement in   the footsteps of the prosody
          suddenly alert   not most

to the remembered verses   tumbling from our mouths
          but to the sudden opening   of minds, of veins of measure

from this impromptu fountain—   *Prufrock*—of all things!—
          rose from us   without bidding

It was no night surely   "of smoky alleys"
          nor was it of "regrets."   Rather a group of rowers

met by chance at night   along the Guadalquivir
          which is at night   black-silver,

strangers hours back   and now no better known,
          and yet: through flowing lines

          words made a bridge

unforeseen. Nothing   to be said but that.

And that a certain hilarity ensued   in all of us, companions . . .
       that kind of night.   Then, the hotel found,

and "good nights" said or sung: rooms were reached
       but, in the way that poetry   makes possible

in the minds of several   (while the bodies
       brushed their teeth   combed hair, opened windows)

the cadences   of the descanted poem
       (like and yet unlike   wine poured out,

like and yet unlike   the Guadalquivir's waters
       heading, unequivocal   where they must)

the rhythms and the haltings   kept coming back and back
       lulling some to sleep,   the river all abandoned,

and others to be curious   wide awake to the murmuring
       and the questions   of the water

A LIGHT

I shone a light behind a slide—
transparency! To see each other young again
perhaps, or, harder, to see us as we were,
or as we thought we were. Do you see, my darling?

I wanted to see our darling days, days before
dark unfurled, days of staring down
two flights into the tiny square—"the garden!"—
at the furious Mr. Murphy and his potatoes.

He could not have been *so* irascible—
he gave us some square feet to work
(about the size of a slide, or of
a memory, penned) gave us those,

And you so happy at your first
and almost only garden, of red (tomatoes),
and green (basil) and blissful scent. It was

a square, a brief catching, yet perfect grasp
of happiness. In that slide,
we both wear green. And though it was fall,

we grinned as if it were spring,
and we permanently awake to the next thing.

CODA: A PHOTO, NOT A SLIDE

Gangly calf, young you: long legs, the stance,
The clods of earth, and Mr. Morphy, as we called him,
Biding his time. A shadow. I was pinned in front of you
By your akimbo arms, your elegant hands.

We laughed like fools. And at dusk
from that small porch we watched the night-
hawks' show. It was enough.

Notes

THE WOMAN AT THE TIJUANA DUMP

Luis Alberto Urrea's *Across the Wire: Life and Hard Times on the Mexican* Border (Anchor Books, 1993) was the first book of the last few decades to shine a bright, provocative, and compassionate light on the city south of the California border, Tijuana, and its economically luckier sibling to the north, San Diego. I am indebted to Luis for my own connection to and with "The Woman at the Tijuana Dump."

The Madams of the Sacred Heart (*Les Dames du Sacre Coeur*) are an order of teaching nuns founded by St. Madeleine Sophie Barat in France in 1800, and dedicated to the education of young women.

UPHOLSTERY

"Tlot-Tlot, Tlot-tlot" was Alfred Noyes's memorable conveying of the sound of galloping horses (both the highwayman's and those of pursuing soldiers) in his classic poetic narrative "The Highwayman." Much read and memorized by children, despite its violence, and the fate of "Bess, the landlord's daughter," it was first published in 1906 in *Blackwood's Magazine*.

GALAXIES

William Carleton's *Traits and Stories of the Irish Peasantry* (1830), as well as his other fictions, are essential reading for students of Anglo-Irish literature of the nineteenth century.

What came to be known as the Battle of the Bogside in Derry, Northern Ireland, occurred between August 12 and 24, 1969. The Tet Offensive began in early 1968 and continued fiercely throughout the summer of that year.

KING PLEASURE, 1976

"King Pleasure" was the birth name of Clarence Beeks (1922-1982). His voice and his matchless vocalese on "Moody's Mood for Love" (by horn player James Moody) were the sources of the imitation sung by the lover in this poem.

Acknowledgments

I wish to thank the editors of the journals where the following poems appeared, sometimes in earlier versions.

Agni	"A Scrap of Fabric at Chatham," "Worlds"
Anglican Theological Review	"Behind the House"
The Atlantic	"Jigsaw," "Patio," "As in the Days of the Prophets," "Central and Main"
Beloit Poetry Journal	"Dream and Precis"
Boston Book Review	"The Straps of their Sandals"
Boston Phoenix	"By Ourselves"
Image	"To Find a Way to the World's Heart"
LEON Literary Review	"Things," "It Was Yeats," "The Siren"
Measure	"March"
Notre Dame Review	"Upholstery"
Orion	"The First to Make Music" (differently titled)
Partisan Review	"The Chosen"
South Dakota Review	"Happiness" (differently titled), "Almost Still Life"
Southwest Review	"The Woman at the Tijuana Dump"
War, Literature & The Arts	"Teaching *To the Lighthouse*"

And, I am deeply grateful to my poets group—Kathleen Aguero, Suzanne Berger, Erica Funkhouser, and Helena Minton—for their assistance, acuity, forbearance and friendship. My thanks as well go to the American Academy in Rome which offered me a place of tranquility and beauty in which to complete this volume and to begin the next.

This book was set in Centaur, designed by the American typographer and book designer, Bruce Rogers, who was commissioned to create an exclusive type for the Metropolitan Museum of Art (New York) in 1914. Based on the Renaissance-period printing of Nicolas Jenson around 1470, it was named Centaur after the title of the first book designed by Rogers using the type: *The Centaur* by Maurice de Guérin, published in 1915. Lanston Monotype of London cut the commercial version of Centaur and released it in 1929.

This book was designed by Shannon Carter, Ian Creeger, and Gregory Wolfe. It was published in hardcover, paperback, and electronic formats by Wipf and Stock Publishers, Eugene, Oregon.

The painting on the cover is *Santo Spirito* by John Lockwood. Collection of the author.

CPSIA information can be obtained
at www.ICGtesting.com
Printed in the USA
BVHW030251131120
593245BV00019B/160

"Love took the words right out of my mouth." So begins the first line of Christopher Jane Corkery's poignant and unforgettable new collection of poems. Throughout the work these two themes—the power and mystery of language, especially the crafted one of poetry, and what Keats called "the holiness of the heart's affections"—intertwine, accumulating a rich panoply of associations and meanings.

The occasions for Corkery's poems are often domestic: the thrill of youthful romance, of marriage and family, of children inventing new worlds. Yet here also are a poet's acts, psychological and spiritual, in a life which, like every reader's life, contains plenty and its absence all at once.

Objects matter here—a bread board, a swing, a still life—but so do places (from New England to Paris and Seville). The poet is also joined by the ghostly presences of poets and mystics, from Teresa of Avila, John Keats, and George Herbert to Emily Dickinson and William Butler Yeats.

Again and again Corkery is drawn to the essential way in which poetry enacts love. In fullness or in scarcity, in loving or in grief, both writer and reader are engaged, fulfilling the contract of poetry.

"In her poem 'Hawthorn and Waxwings' Corkery looks lovingly at what these birds, fellow creatures, do, working hard at those trembling berries, to ward off death, and in her other poems she looks as lovingly at what other fellow creatures do. Corkery has said about how these poems look at our fellow creatures: 'We were storing love in our cells for a reason.' I love this book."
—DAVID FERRY, author of *Bewilderment: New Poems and Translations*

"Beneath a modest surface these poems struggle with all the big questions—and then have the courage to end in defeat. 'No answer, no answer,' concludes 'By the Ocean'; and yet somehow that is an answer, and a satisfying one at that. Meanwhile Corkery offers the particularities of ongoing life as our best alternative. A dry riverbed in Tuscany, waxwings eating hawthorn berries in a magical miniature—this is what we can have instead of answers. These poems, at once wry, frank, and heartbroken, balance on the knife's edge between light and dark."
—LINDA BAMBER, author of *Metropolitan Tang*

"What binds together Christopher Jane Corkery's new collection of poems? Memory without nostalgia, grief without self-pity, sirens, laughter and—from start to finish—a formally adept and musical ear. It has been too many years since *Blessing*, her remarkable first book, and now we see that it has been worth the wait."
—LEWIS HYDE, author of *The Gift*

CHRISTOPHER JANE CORKERY'S first collection, *Blessing*, was published in the Princeton Series of Contemporary Poetry. Her poems have appeared in *Agni*, *The Atlantic*, *Image*, *Kenyon Review*, and elsewhere. The winner of a Pushcart Prize, she has received an Ingram Merrill Foundation Fellowship and has been a fellow of Yaddo and the MacDowell Colony. Recently a Visiting Artist at the American Academy in Rome, she taught for many years at the College of the Holy Cross.

ISBN 978-1-7252-6421-2

SLANT

An imprint of *Wipf and Stock Publishers*
slantbooks.com | wipfandstock.com

9 781725 264212